JULIAN ASSANGE
FOUNDER OF WIKILEAKS

BY RACHEL MORITZ

CONTENT CONSULTANT
Hannah Gurman, Clinical Associate Professor
New York University

Core Library

An Imprint of Abdo Publishing
abdopublishing.com

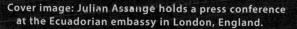

Cover image: Julian Assange holds a press conference
at the Ecuadorian embassy in London, England.

abdopublishing.com

Published by Abdo Publishing, a division of ABDO, PO Box 398166, Minneapolis, Minnesota 55439. Copyright © 2018 by Abdo Consulting Group, Inc. International copyrights reserved in all countries. No part of this book may be reproduced in any form without written permission from the publisher. Core Library™ is a trademark and logo of Abdo Publishing.

Printed in the United States of America, North Mankato, Minnesota
052017
092017

Cover Photo: John Stillwell/AP Images
Interior Photos: John Stillwell/AP Images, 1; Chris Radburn/AP Images, 4–5; Sterba Martin/CTK/Alamy, 7; Shutterstock Images, 10–11; Wenn Ltd/Alamy, 12; Sascha Steinbach/Getty Images News/Getty Images, 14; Guy Corbishley/Alamy, 16–17; iStockphoto, 19; Rich Bowen/Alamy, 20, 45; Jeff Gilbert/Alamy, 23; Kokkai Ng/iStockphoto, 24–25; Zuma Press Inc/Alamy, 27; Photononstop/SuperStock, 28; Chris Baston/Alamy, 30; Fred Mack/Alamy, 32–33; Patrick Semansky/AP Images, 34; Rupert Hartley/Rex Features/AP Images, 37; Dominic Lipinski/Press Association/URN:29167219/AP Images, 40

Editor: Alyssa Krekelberg
Imprint Designer: Maggie Villaume
Series Design Direction: Maggie Villaume

Publisher's Cataloging-in-Publication Data

Names: Moritz, Rachel, author.
Title: Julian Assange : founder of WikiLeaks / by Rachel Moritz.
Other titles: Founder of WikiLeaks
Description: Minneapolis, MN : Abdo Publishing, 2018. | Series: Newsmakers | Includes bibliographical references and index.
Identifiers: LCCN 2017930436 | ISBN 9781532111792 (lib. bdg.) | ISBN 9781680789645 (ebook)
Subjects: LCSH: Assange, Julian--Juvenile literature. | WikiLeaks (Organization)--Juvenile literature. | Editors--Australia--Biography--Juvenile literature. | Publishers and publishing--Biography--Juvenile literature. | Radicals--Juvenile literature. | Leaks (Disclosure of information)--Political aspects--Juvenile literature. | Official secrets--Juvenile literature. | Whistle blowing Political aspects--Juvenile literature.
Classification: DDC 070.92 [B]--dc23
LC record available at http://lccn.loc.gov/2017930436

CONTENTS

CHAPTER ONE

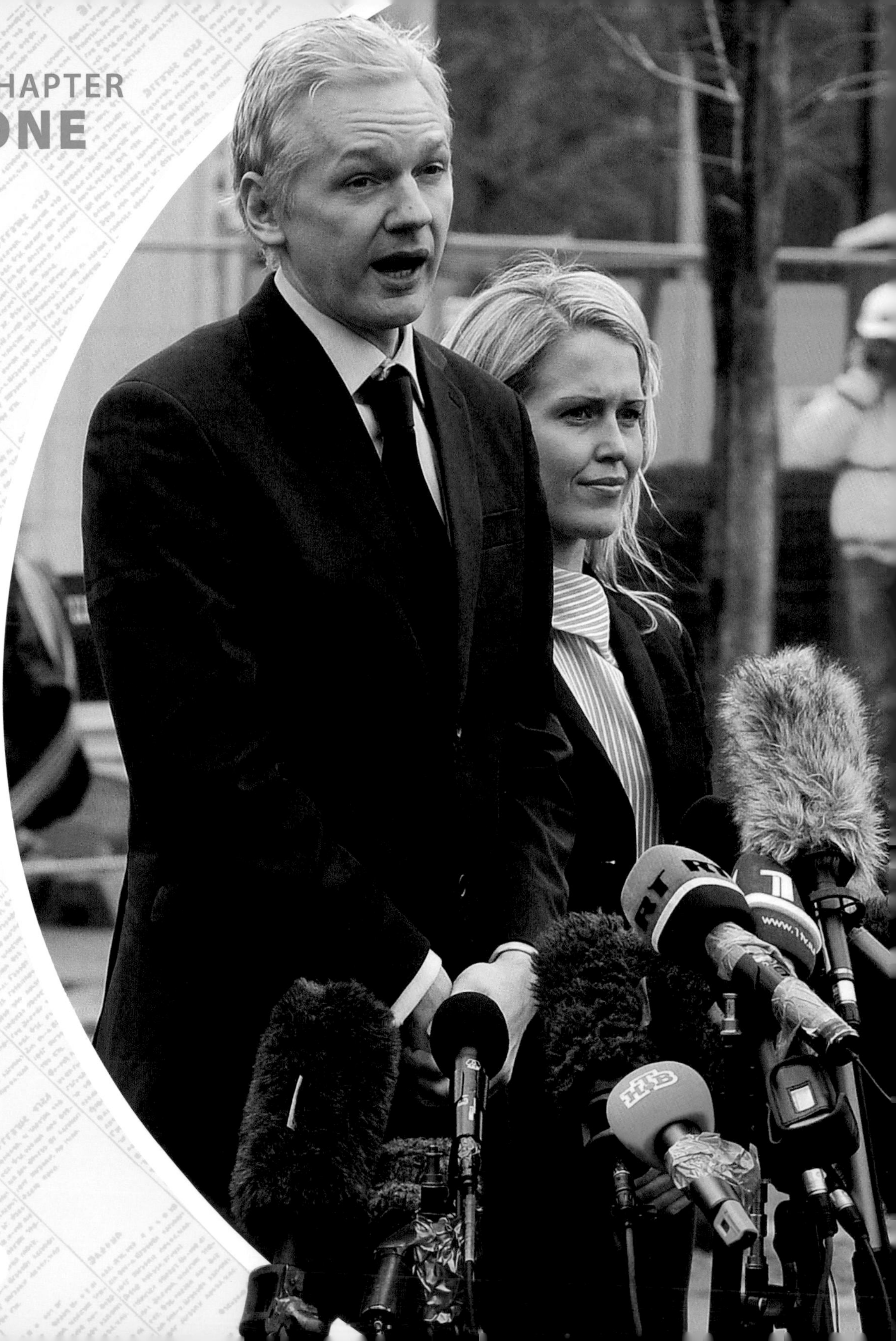

DOES THE WORLD NEED WIKILEAKS?

The crowd clapped as Julian Assange took his seat at the TEDGlobal Conference in Oxford, England. It was July 2010. The audience was ready to hear him talk about his famous website, WikiLeaks. He had created the site four years earlier. Now, Assange was ready to talk about why he believed the world needed WikiLeaks.

WikiLeaks publishes secret documents, photos, and videos online. Many of these things come from people working for governments or corporations. They

Julian Assange publishes secret documents on his website, WikiLeaks.

anonymously send these materials to the site. These individuals are known as whistle-blowers. Sometimes they think the organization they work for is doing something wrong. They believe the public has a right to know about the secret materials they send to WikiLeaks. Assange believes this too.

Under the bright stage lights, Assange explained why he believes WikiLeaks is important. He said the documents published on WikiLeaks have information people should know about. Under Assange's leadership, WikiLeaks has released more secret documents than

A FAMOUS WHISTLE-BLOWER

One of Assange's heroes is a man named Daniel Ellsberg. In 1971 Ellsberg sent a reporter at the *New York Times* US government documents about the Vietnam War (1954–1975). These papers were classified. That means they held government secrets. Ellsberg went to trial for leaking the papers. However, he was not sent to jail. Today Ellsberg is known as a famous whistle-blower. His actions made people wonder whether the United States should take its soldiers out of Vietnam.

WikiLeaks has released thousands of documents online.

any other news source. Assange started the WikiLeaks website in 2006. Since then the website has posted thousands of controversial documents. Because of some information published on WikiLeaks, Assange is under investigation by the US government.

A CONTROVERSIAL FIGURE

Assange's website has sparked debates on whether or not WikiLeaks does more harm than good. Assange's supporters say WikiLeaks is used to defend free

THE POWER OF A WIKI

WikiLeaks began as an online wiki. A wiki is a type of website that can be accessed and edited by anyone. Volunteer writers post entries. In addition, they fact-check each other. Articles do not rely on a single expert or editor. However, Assange realized he could not post everything sent his way. Some information was too sensitive. Other information might not be real. Today, Assange and his staff look at every source posted on WikiLeaks. They also destroy information about their sources. That way no one can discover who sent them the information.

speech. Critics of the website say Assange puts people's lives at risk when he leaks secret stories. The US government has said certain documents published on WikiLeaks are a threat to the country's security. Today, people across the globe turn to WikiLeaks for information. Journalists use the website as a source for their stories. Assange views himself as a journalist and activist. Growing up, he was a hacker and computer programmer.

STRAIGHT TO THE
SOURCE

In 2010 Assange was interviewed by *Time* magazine about the value of WikiLeaks. He talked about why his organization keeps the identities of its sources secret. In the interview, Assange discussed who has the right to keep secrets:

> *We keep secret the identity of our sources . . . [and] take great pains to do it. Secrecy is important for many things but shouldn't be used to cover up abuses. . . . It shouldn't really be that people are thinking about, "Should something be secret?" I would rather it be thought, "Who has a responsibility to keep certain things secret?" And, "Who has a responsibility to bring matters to the public?" And those responsibilities fall on different players. And it is our responsibility to bring matters to the public.*

Source: "*Time*'s Julian Assange Interview: Full Transcript/Audio." *Time Magazine*. Time, Inc. December 1, 2010. Web. Accessed September 27, 2016.

Back It Up

In this passage, Assange describes how he thinks differently about government secrets and the secret identities of WikiLeaks' sources. Write a paragraph summarizing Assange's feelings about how these two kinds of secrets are different. Use evidence from the interview and from Chapter One.

CHAPTER
TWO

GROWING UP

Julian was born in Townsville, Australia, on July 3, 1971. His mother, Christine Hawkins, was strong-willed and artistic. At the age of 17 she ran away from home. She sold her artwork to buy a motorcycle and a tent. She met Julian's father, John Shipton, at a protest against the Vietnam war. Their relationship did not last long. It ended before Julian was born. Later, his mother married an actor named Brett Assange. The family moved from town to town with Assange's theater company. Julian learned to set up theater spotlights and audio equipment by the time he was five years old.

Townsville is located in the northeastern part of Australia.

Christine Hawkins raised Julian Assange in Australia.

When Julian was nine, his mother divorced Assange. She then married a musician named Keith Hamilton. They had a son together. But Hamilton was part of an Australian group known for mistreating young children. Hawkins feared for her sons' safety. She ran away from her husband in 1982. For the next five years, the family moved across Australia. Hamilton followed them. Julian learned to pack his suitcase quickly. They moved from house to house. Sometimes Hawkins even changed her sons' names. No one felt safe until members of the group were arrested in 1987. Finally, the family settled outside of Melbourne, Australia. By the time he turned 14, Julian had attended at least 12 different schools.

COMPUTER WHIZ KID

Julian did not seem to mind his family's traveling. He liked to spend time alone. He struggled to get along with children at school. Julian loved to fish, build rafts, ride horses, and explore the outdoors.

EARLY HACKERS

Computer hacking began in the 1960s. Hackers can manipulate computer code. Code is a set of symbols computers can understand. In the 1970s and 1980s some computer hackers began doing things that were against the law. They tapped into phone lines and made free long-distance calls. Others broke into protected computer systems over the Internet and stole information.

Julian showed interest in computers at a young age. When he was 11 years old, he began visiting a

Commodore 64 computers were released in 1982.

nearby electronics shop. Julian learned how to write his first computer program on the shop's Commodore 64 computer. In 1987, when he was 16 years old, Julian's mother bought him his very own Commodore 64.

Julian spent hours developing his computer skills. He taught himself how to program. This skill allowed him to give computers instructions to perform tasks. Julian used his programming skills to hack into nearby computer systems, such as Australia's Royal Melbourne Institute of Technology. He was interested in learning how these systems worked. Years later, his curiosity would get him into trouble with the law.

EXPLORE ONLINE

Chapter Two talks about how new computer technology interested Assange. The website below shows a 1983 advertisement for the Commodore 64. How is the information from the advertisement the same as the information in Chapter Two? What new information did you learn from the advertisement?

COMMODORE 64 ADVERTISEMENT
abdocorelibrary.com/julian-assange

CHAPTER
THREE

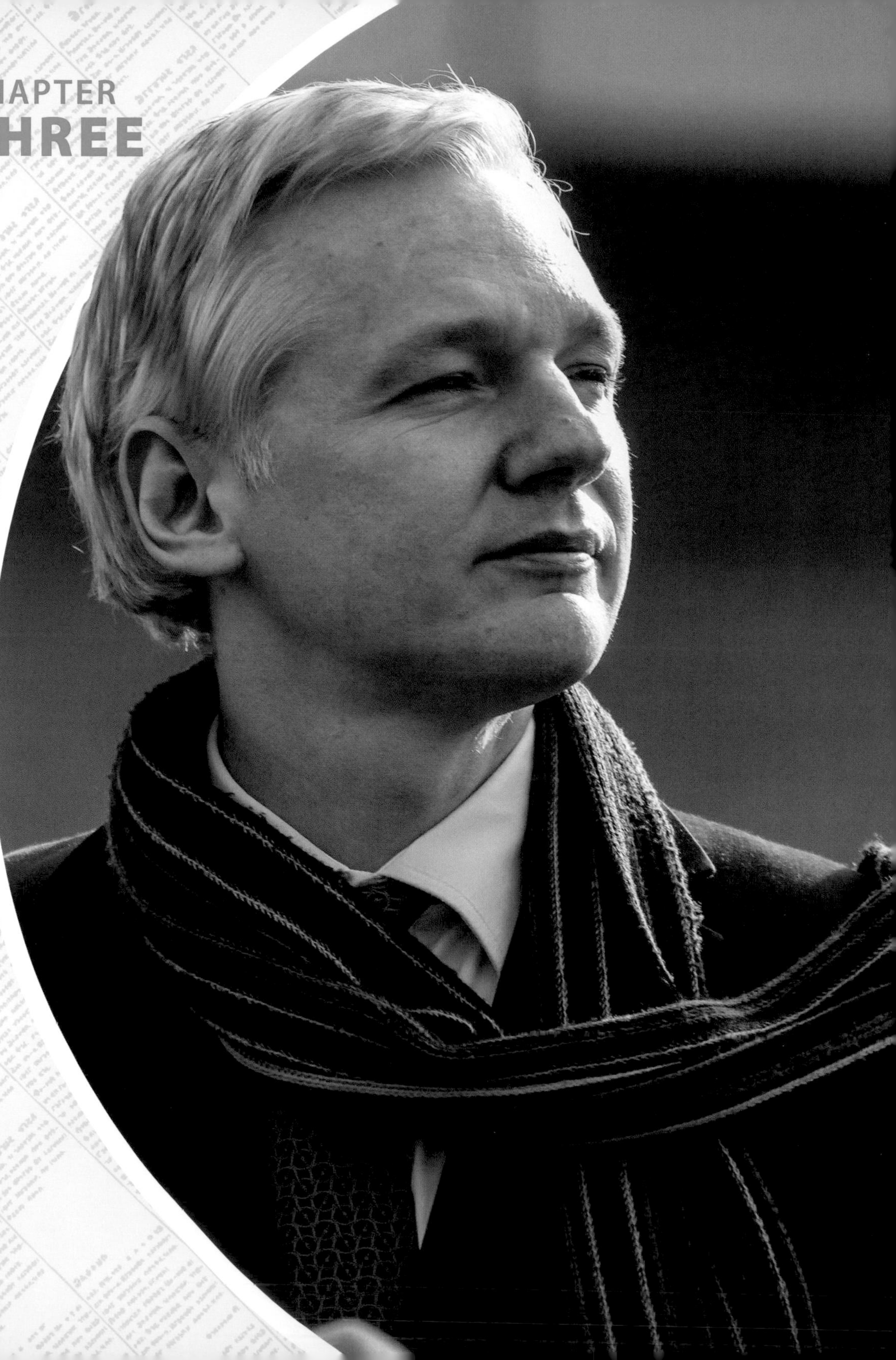

A YOUNG COMPUTER HACKER

I n 1988 Assange turned 18. He married his high school girlfriend, Teresa. They had a son named Daniel. At this time, with two friends, Assange formed a hacker group called the International Subversives. Each member of the group had a special hacker name. Assange's name was Mendax, which means "nobly untruthful" in Latin.

Late at night, they used their computers and coding skills to illegally break into computer systems all over the world. Assange said hacking was addictive. It took up much of

Julian Assange helped form a hacker group.

ASSANGE'S BIG BREAK

At age 17, Assange had his first big hacking success. He broke into a large computer system called Minerva. This system belonged to the government-owned telecommunications company in Sydney, Australia. To hack Minerva, Assange needed a password. To get the password, he pretended to be a worker calling from his office. Assange called the company's headquarters. The man Assange called believed he was an office worker and told him the password. Soon he was inside the system.

his time. With his skills, he could gain access to large networks and control them.

A COMPUTER WORM

Assange and his friends were looking for new hacking challenges. So they decided to target computer systems at the United States' National Aeronautics and Space Administration (NASA). Like many people in the late 1980s, Assange worried about nuclear war. The United States and the Soviet Union had thousands of

The International Subversives broke into the NASA computer system.

nuclear weapons. Around the world, people marched in the streets to protest. They wanted governments to stop making nuclear weapons.

In October 1989, NASA was ready to launch a new spacecraft. It contained nuclear fuel. People worried the spacecraft would blow up and spill the nuclear fuel. In Melbourne, Assange and the International Subversives prepared to illegally hack into NASA's system.

Minutes before the spacecraft's launch, a message appeared on NASA computer screens. It said hackers had broken into the system. The International Subversives had released a computer program. It was called a worm. It spread quickly from computer to computer. It deleted files and passwords.

Eventually, the launch took place with no other problems. However, federal police began investigating the computer worm. They suspected it came from Australia.

Julian Assange has been under investigation multiple times.

A LIFE DISSOLVING

The year 1991 was difficult for Assange. The police were after him and his personal life was falling apart. Assange spent hours hacking at night. His wife did not like the amount of time he spent at his computer. She worried about the dangers of hacking. Eventually, she filed for divorce. Assange became depressed. He was not as careful covering his steps during his nighttime hacking. His depression may have affected how quickly the police tracked him down.

POLICE ON HIS TRAIL

Assange continued hacking. He broke into systems at a Canadian telecommunications company. He also hacked into US military computer systems. Assange did not damage the systems he hacked into. However, his actions were against the law.

The police suspected Assange. They listened to his phone calls. They searched his house in October 1991. Eventually, Assange confessed to computer hacking.

Assange's criminal investigation went on for several years. In 1996 he went to court in Australia. He pleaded guilty to 24 counts of hacking. The judge thought his

Julian Assange would face trial again in 2011.

actions were very serious. However, he decided that
Assange had acted out of curiosity and meant no harm.
The judge fined him $2,100. He warned him to stop
hacking. Assange had avoided jail and was allowed to
go free.

CHAPTER FOUR

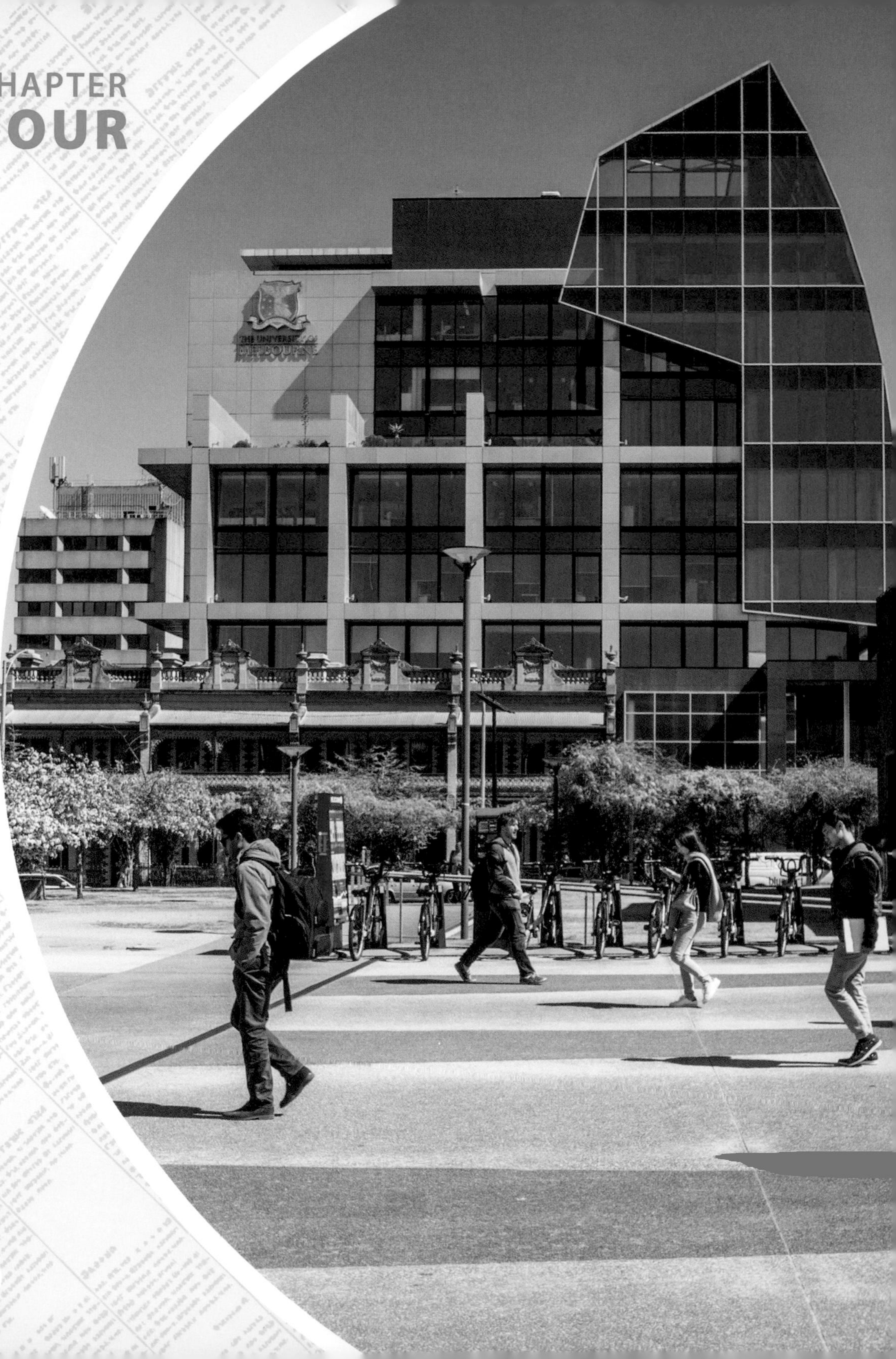

THE LAUNCH OF WIKILEAKS

After his trial for computer hacking, Assange spent many years out of the public eye. He studied math and physics at the University of Melbourne. But Assange never lost his passion for computers. The 1990s were an exciting time for computer development. The rise of the Internet and the World Wide Web let people communicate with each other across the globe.

In 2006 Assange decided to start a website. He wanted the website to share important information. He also wanted the website to support human rights struggles. He named the website WikiLeaks. Assange

Julian Assange went to school at the University of Melbourne in Australia.

25

THE WORLD WIDE WEB AND INTERNET

In 1989 British computer scientist Tim Berners-Lee invented the World Wide Web. The Web is a large collection of documents, called web pages. Web pages are interconnected. They contain sections of clickable text that take users to related pages. The World Wide Web and Internet are not the same thing. The Internet is a large network of connected computers. The World Wide Web is the collection of web pages found on these computers.

gathered volunteers to run the website. They began receiving millions of documents from different countries. In December 2006, the website posted its first leaked document online. WikiLeaks was live.

HIGH-PROFILE LEAKS

By 2008 WikiLeaks had posted many leaked documents. Journalists began using WikiLeaks as a news source. Assange faced his first challenge when WikiLeaks published a report called "Cry of Blood." It came from a human rights group in Kenya, a country in East Africa.

Julian Assange has received criticism for his website.

WIKILEAKS AND
THE WORLD

The WikiLeaks logo looks like two sides of an hourglass holding the world's continents. Chapter Four explains what Assange wants WikiLeaks to accomplish. What do you think the logo expresses about the work WikiLeaks aims to do?

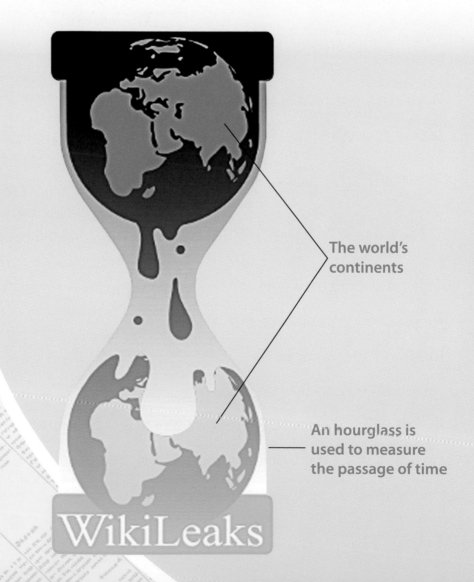

The world's continents

An hourglass is used to measure the passage of time

WikiLeaks

The document stated that the Kenyan government had murdered up to 500 people. After the report was published on WikiLeaks, two human rights activists in Kenya were killed. People around the world said Assange and WikiLeaks had exposed the activists. They believed the information on WikiLeaks led to the activists' deaths.

Across the globe, WikiLeaks was involved in another big story. This time the story was focused on a bank. In 2008 Iceland faced financial trouble. Major Icelandic banks could no longer pay the money they owed. A WikiLeaks document showed that one bank had loaned away billions of dollars of its customers'

WHAT'S A CORPORATION?

Assange wanted WikiLeaks to challenge corporations as well as governments. The two share some things in common. Like governments, corporations are formed by a group of people. They appoint leaders to make decisions. But a corporation's main goal is to make money. Because of this, Assange believes corporations can overstep their power to make money.

People across the world can access WikiLeaks.

money. People working at the banks tried to keep reporters from writing about what was happening. However, people were able to visit the WikiLeaks website to learn the truth. People began demanding better government control over banks. They also wanted more freedom of the press. Two years after its creation, the WikiLeaks website was impacting people and governments.

STRAIGHT TO THE
SOURCE

In December 2006, WikiLeaks sent an e-mail to individuals it hoped would join it. It described how it believed WikiLeaks would support good governance around the world:

> *Our primary targets are those highly oppressive regimes in China, Russia and central Eurasia. . . . We believe fostering a safe, easy, socially sanctified way for uncensorable mass document leaking, publishing and analysis is THE most cost effective generator of good governance. We seek good governance, because good governance does more than run trains on time. Good governance responds to the sufferings of its people. Good governance answers injustice.*

Source: Valierie Guichaoua. *Julian Assange–Wikileaks: Warrior for Truth*. Quebec, Canada: Cogito Media Group, 2011. Print. 125–126.

What's the Big Idea?

In this e-mail, WikiLeaks shares its plan to target governments and corporations. Why does WikiLeaks encourage people to reveal unethical behavior by governments and corporations? What benefit does it believe this will have? Use supporting details from this source.

CHAPTER **FIVE**

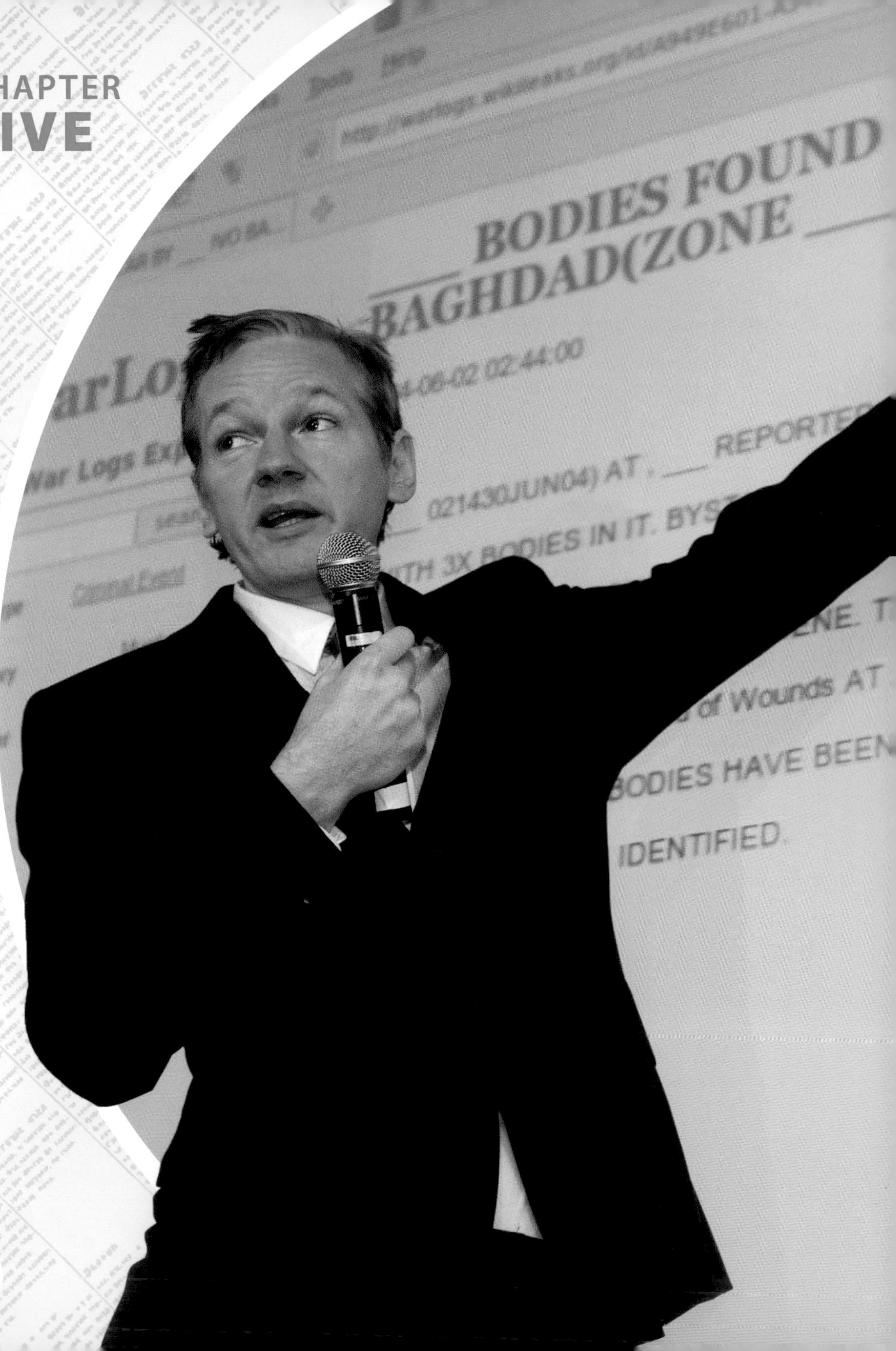

PUBLISHING WAR SECRETS

n 2010 Assange received his biggest leak yet. It came from a US soldier stationed in Iraq, a country in the Middle East. The soldier sent WikiLeaks more than 700,000 classified documents and videos. At the time, this was the biggest leak in US military history.

Assange's source was a 20-year-old soldier then named Bradley Manning. For months Manning served in Iraq. He read documents and reports showing the ugliness of war. He learned many women and children had been killed during US military attacks in Afghanistan, a country in Central Asia. He read about

Julian Assange explains the release of classified war documents.

Bradley Manning was arrested for leaking classified documents to WikiLeaks.

prisoners who were tortured in Iraq and at the political prison in Guantánamo Bay, Cuba.

Manning believed the public should know these things were happening. He began sending classified files to WikiLeaks. These leaked documents revealed secret reports about the United States' wars in

Iraq and Afghanistan. Manning was arrested by the US military. He went to trial for sharing military documents. Manning was sentenced to 35 years in prison. Around this time, Manning announced she identified as a woman, taking the name Chelsea instead. Years later, President Barack Obama reduced her prison sentence. She was released in 2017.

After this leak, Assange's name appeared in world newspapers. He was interviewed on television. In Washington, DC, US government officials began investigating WikiLeaks. They stated the leaked documents

VIDEO EVIDENCE

One of Manning's leaks showed a video taken by a US helicopter. On the morning of July 12, 2007, crew members on board two helicopters killed 12 people in the streets of Iraq. Two journalists were killed in the attack. Two young children were also wounded. The video showed how soldiers had mistaken the journalists' cameras for weapons. Many people felt it showed a war crime. This video aired on television. It was the most famous of Manning's leaks.

put the country's security at risk. Political leaders also said the information on WikiLeaks threatened people's safety in Afghanistan and Iraq.

UNDER INVESTIGATION

In August 2010, Assange traveled to Stockholm, Sweden. During his ten-day stay, two women accused Assange of assaulting them. Assange said the charges were false. He left Sweden and went to England. Assange refused to return to Sweden for questioning. He claimed Swedish officials would send him to the United States. He thought he would face trial for publishing the country's war documents.

In 2012 Assange reached out to the government of Ecuador. He wanted to stay at the Ecuadorian embassy in London, England. That way the British government couldn't arrest him. The Ecuadorian embassy agreed. Assange moved into a room with a bed, telephone, computer, shower, treadmill, and small kitchen.

Julian Assange believed he would be arrested if he left the Ecuadorian embassy.

By the spring of 2017, Assange was still running WikiLeaks from inside.

2016 DEMOCRATIC PARTY CANDIDATES

US presidential elections are held every four years. During election season, political parties pick a candidate they want to run for president. The two major political parties are the Democratic and Republican parties. In 2016 the Democratic Party had to pick between candidates Hillary Clinton and Bernie Sanders.

HEADLINE MAKER

Today, WikiLeaks continues to release sensitive documents. The information published on the website has caused political arguments within the United States. One incident involved the 2016 presidential election between Hillary Clinton and Donald Trump. WikiLeaks published hacked e-mails from the Democratic National Committee. These e-mails suggested the Democratic Party unfairly favored Clinton over her fellow Democratic opponent, Bernie Sanders. Many people

LEAKED
DOCUMENTS

This chart includes some of the best-known WikiLeaks stories. Do you believe Assange was right in publishing this secret information? Why might people be interested in learning about the information in these documents?

YEAR	NAME	DESCRIPTION
2010	The Iraq War Logs	These leaked files contained classified US military documents from the US war in Iraq. Some documents revealed unreported Iraqi civilian deaths.
2010	Collateral Murder	Classified video footage showed the shooting of Iraqi civilians by the US military.
2011	Guantánamo Files	WikiLeaks published secret files about the US detention camp in Guantánamo Bay, Cuba. These files showed the unfair treatment of prisoners.
2015–16	Trade in Services Agreement	WikiLeaks published details of secret trade deal negotiations between the United States, the European Union, and 22 other countries around the world.
2016	Erdogan AKP Leaks	WikiLeaks released e-mails from the Turkish government aimed at exposing its leaders' corruption.

Julian Assange talks to the media from the Ecuadorian embassy's balcony.

accused WikiLeaks of trying to influence the election. Clinton eventually lost the election to Trump.

Critics of WikiLeaks claim the website is not focused on exposing human rights issues. They say WikiLeaks has become selective about the countries it targets. Some critics have said WikiLeaks focuses too much on the United States.

Assange has expressed disapproval of the United States. He claims the country punishes people who tell the truth. Assange has not criticized other countries as loudly as he has the United States. People have questioned why Assange does not leak more documents from Russia, even though its government has unlawfully jailed people and has control over the country's media and Internet.

Assange remains a controversial figure. His website has changed the way people think about secret information. Today, many important stories continue to play out online at WikiLeaks.

FURTHER EVIDENCE

Chapter Five has information about Chelsea Manning sending US war documents to WikiLeaks. What is one of the main points in this chapter? The website at the link below discusses Manning's prison sentence. Find a quote from the website. Does the information on the website support the main point of the chapter? Does it present new evidence?

CHELSEA MANNING TO BE RELEASED EARLY AS OBAMA COMMUTES SENTENCE
abdocorelibrary.com/julian-assange

IMPORTANT DATES

1971
Julian Assange is born on July 3.

1987
Assange receives his first computer, a Commodore 64.

1989
Assange is believed to be involved with a computer worm that temporarily shuts down a NASA spacecraft launch.

1996
Assange is charged with 24 counts of computer hacking.

2006
Assange starts the website WikiLeaks.

2008
WikiLeaks publishes documents about human rights abuses in Kenya and bank fraud in Iceland.

2010

WikiLeaks publishes classified US war documents. The Swedish government issues a warrant for Assange's arrest.

2012

Assange seeks asylum at the Ecuadorian embassy in London, England.

2016

WikiLeaks publishes e-mails from the Democratic National Committee, which causes controversy in the 2016 US presidential election.

STOP AND
THINK

You Are There

Chapter Five discusses Chelsea (formerly Bradley) Manning's leak of classified US military documents. Imagine you are a soldier like Manning who has come to believe your country is involved in an unjust war. Write a letter home telling your friends what this feels like. Be sure to add plenty of detail to your notes.

Tell the Tale

Chapters Four and Five of this book talk about Assange publishing government secrets. Imagine you work at a newspaper and receive secret information from WikiLeaks. Write 200 words on whether you would print this information, and explain why or why not.

Dig Deeper

After reading this book, what questions do you still have about Assange? With an adult's help, find a few reliable sources that can help you answer your questions. Write a paragraph about what you learned.

Take a Stand

Chapter Three describes how Assange and his friends illegally hacked into computer systems. When Assange went to trial in Australia, he did not receive a prison sentence. Imagine that you are the judge ruling on Assange's case. Would you make the same decision? Write a paragraph arguing your opinion on the issue. Support your argument with evidence from this book.

GLOSSARY

activist
someone who works toward a political cause or belief

assault
a violent physical attack

classified
kept secret

controversial
giving rise to public disagreement

critics
people who express a negative opinion of something

regime
a government in power

security
the protection of a country against illegal activity

source
a person, book, or website from whom a journalist receives information

whistle-blowers
people who expose information or activities that may be wrong or against the law

LEARN MORE

Books

Bedell, Jane. *So, You Want to Be a Coder.* New York: Beyond Words/Aladdin, 2016.

Idzikowski, Lisa. *Computer Science in the Real World.* Minneapolis, MN: Abdo Publishing, 2016.

Woodcock, Jon. *Coding Games in Scratch.* New York: DK, 2016.

Websites

To learn more about Newsmakers, visit **abdobooklinks.com**. These links are routinely monitored and updated to provide the most current information available.

Visit **abdocorelibrary.com** for free additional tools for teachers and students.

INDEX

About the Author

Rachel Moritz is a freelance writer and the author of two books of poetry. She lives with her partner and son in Minneapolis, Minnesota.